BERTRAND RUSSELL IN 90 MINUTES

Bertrand Russell
IN 90 MINUTES

Paul Strathern

IVAN R. DEE
CHICAGO

Library of Congress Cataloging-in-Publication Data:
Strathern, Paul, 1940–
    Bertrand Russell in 90 minutes / Paul Strathern.
      p. cm.
    Includes bibliographical references and index.
    ISBN 1-56663-356-7 (alk. paper) — ISBN 1-56663-357-5
(pbk. : alk. paper)
    1. Russell, Bertrand, 1872–1970. I. Title: Bertrand Russell
in ninety minutes. II. Title.

B1649.R94 S77 2001
192—dc21
[B]   00-065843

Contents

BERTRAND RUSSELL IN 90 MINUTES

Introduction

Bertrand Russell lived for almost ninety-eight years. It was a long and remarkably eventful life for a philosopher, and it covered the greatest century of change which humanity has so far witnessed. When Russell was born, the American Civil War had just finished, and the twenty-eight-year-old Nietzsche was writing his first book, *The Birth of Tragedy*. By the time Russell died, man had set foot on the moon, and even the philosopher who succeeded to his mantle, Wittgenstein, had been dead for almost a quarter of a century.

Russell asserted that throughout his life he was driven by three great passions—the longing for love, the quest for knowledge, and heart-rending pity for the suffering of humanity. He sought the first in order to escape an unendurable loneliness, and because the ecstasy it brought him was so great he claimed he would willingly have sacrificed his life for such bliss. His pursuit of knowledge was equally passionate. He needed to know "why the stars shine" and the power "by which numbers hold sway above the flux." His philosophy always took deep account of science, a necessity that eluded many philosophers during a century in which science transformed the world. Darwin's theory of evolution was still new when Russell was born; the unraveling of the structure of DNA was under way by the time he died. In between, relativity, quantum physics, nuclear fission, and the Big Bang theory had changed forever the way we viewed our universe.

Yet in many ways Russell's philosophical outlook—deeply rooted as it was in both logic and empiricism—remained essentially unchanged. For the most part his manner was both lucid and commonsensical, though he would characterize common sense itself as "the metaphysics of savages," and refused to let the content of his thought (as distinct from its mode of expression) be distorted by its malign influence. Russell was aristocratic enough not to mind appearing ludicrous. Indeed, a number of his more extreme political stances were largely viewed as just this. His character was a potent mix of elitist arrogance, candid honesty, and unbending principle. He could see into the depths of the world (both philosophically and politically), but he was often blind concerning his own inner world. Yet it was this psychological unknowingness which appeared to drive him, giving emotional force to even his most intellectual inquiries as well as his frequent affairs of the heart.

A passionate approach indeed for a philosopher, this driven quest for love and knowledge. As Russell himself acknowledged, such pursuits led him toward the heavens. Yet it was his third passion, his pity for suffering humanity, that brought him back to earth. The victims of the world's human-inflicted evils—war, poverty, torture, pain—would again and again stir him to quixotic action.

Throughout his life Russell remained a figure of contradiction and controversy. The man who was for a period regarded as the world's leading philosopher would also be reviled for his advanced liberal views on love and other social matters. The man who was honored with the Nobel Prize was also twice sent to jail. The man who sought to establish a demonstrably certain logical philosophy would encourage the very philosopher whose work superseded and undermined this philosophy.

Yet if Russell's logical philosophy can be said to have failed, his political philosophy arguably succeeded. (No matter that philosophers regarded the latter as philosophically trivial, or even outrageous: he certainly did not.) Nowadays the accepted social mores of the Western world much more closely resemble Russell's liberal ideas than those of many more widely regarded contemporary political and ethical thinkers. Likewise, his vehement campaign against nuclear weapons laid the foundations for nuclear disarmament—though he would doubtless point out that this process remains far from complete and may still result in the disaster he sought to avoid.

Ultimately Russell himself admitted that he made his greatest efforts in the field of traditional philosophy—in epistemology, the search for the ultimate grounds of our knowledge about the world. How can we be certain that what we claim to know is true? Where lies the certainty in our experience of the world? Can even the most precise knowledge—such as mathematics—be said to rest on any sure logical foundation? These were the questions that Russell sought to answer during the periods of his most profound philosophical thinking. They have remained the perennial questions of philosophy from Plato and Aristotle through Descartes, Hume, and Kant, to Russell and Wittgenstein.

The latter half of the twentieth century saw a concerted attempt to undermine such questions. ("There is no such thing as universal truth." "All knowledge is relative to the historical era or culture in which it is accepted.") But the persistence of scientific-philosophical thinking ensures that the questions Russell addressed remain very much central to present-day thought. His thinking, and the advances he made in epistemology, remain utterly relevant to our contemporary philosophical situation. The age of seemingly ever-expanding scientific knowledge requires more than ever a philosophy to underpin that knowledge. In an overall sense this has yet to be found. Possibly it never will be. Yet the attempt to see how such a philosophy *might* support our scientific knowledge remains fruitful. In trying to discover its certainty we understand more about what such knowledge is. We think scientifically about an apparently scientific world. What does this mean about us and about the world we inhabit? What is the link between these two disparate entities, if any? Russell's thought was one of the later, and more illuminating, stages in this age-old philosophical quest.

Russell's Life and Works

Bertrand Russell was born in 1872 into one of the most distinguished aristocratic families in England. This was the height of the Victorian era, when the British Empire was approaching its apogee. Hypocrisy was the order of the day, amidst widespread social and psychological repression. However, both Russell's parents held enlightened liberal views—his father lost his seat in Parliament for espousing the cause of birth control.

Young Bertrand's childhood was overshadowed by death. Both his parents, and his sister, died by the time he was five. His parents had instructed that their two sons be placed under the guardianship of an atheist friend, but this was contested in the courts by young Bertrand's powerful grandfather, Lord Russell, who had twice been prime minister. The court overruled the parents' will, so Bertrand and his older brother were taken to live with Lord and Lady Russell at Pembroke Lodge in Richmond Park, on the outskirts of London. Queen Victoria herself wrote to congratulate Lady Russell, adding, "I trust that your grandsons will grow up all that you could wish." (As Bertrand Russell wryly commented many years later, this wish "was denied her.") Within a year Lord Russell himself was dead. Young Bertrand lay in bed dreading the moment when Lady Russell too would die, an event that he childishly assumed was bound to happen soon. He focused his mind on the thought of his beloved parents, a fading picture of certainty, sweetness, and light.

Life at Pembroke Lodge was very different. Lady Russell was a willful puritan, though paradoxically she retained the liberal political views of her husband. Her "angel child," as she called Bertrand, was brought up under a regime of cold baths before breakfast and blinkered morality. Such matters as sex and trade were simply not mentioned. Lady Russell decided that her angel should remain uncontaminated by contact with other children. He was educated at home by tutors, with occasional lessons from his amiable elder brother Frank, who was seven years Bertrand's senior and evidently considered a lost cause, for he was sent away to school.

It was Frank who introduced Bertrand to the subject that would transform his life. Russell describes how at the age of eleven he began studying geometry under his brother's tuition. They started working their way through Euclid's *Elements*, and, in Russell's telling words, "I had not imagined there was anything so delicious in the world." Even when they came to Euclid's difficult fifth proposition, Russell found no difficulty, prompting a surprised comment from Frank. Again in Russell's own words: "This was the first time it had dawned upon me that I might have some intelligence." In his isolation he had simply had no one with whom to compare himself. But for the adolescent Bertrand this was something more than the rapturous discovery of some hitherto undreamed-of wonder. The way that Russell regarded mathematics was characteristically original from the start. Frank explained to Bertrand that Euclid had established the whole of geometry by proof, thus making its theorems utterly certain and incontestable. But Bertrand was disappointed to discover that Euclid had in fact based his geometry upon a series of basic axioms. What about proofs for these? Frank replied that there weren't any. Bertrand obstinately refused to go on until Frank produced some. Frank explained to Bertrand that he just had to accept these axioms or they would not be able to progress further. Because Bertrand was dying to learn more of this wonderful geometry, he reluctantly accepted. This love of the formal beauty and certainty of mathematics, as well as the pressing desire for these to be based upon some bedrock of unquestionable truth, would keep Russell alive for the next thirty years.

This is no fanciful exaggeration. Russell's life at Pembroke Lodge remained unhealthily solitary, his feelings for his fellow human beings almost entirely sublimated. He relates how he would frequently go into the garden to look down over Richmond Park and the far vista of the Thames valley. Here he would gaze at the sunset and think about committing suicide. The only thing that prevented him from taking his life was the wish to discover more about the "delicious" abstract beauty of mathematics. He explains how he was searching "for something beyond what the world contains, something transfigured and infinite . . . it's like a passionate love for a ghost. . . . I have always desired to find some justification for the emotions inspired by certain things that seemed to stand outside human life and to deserve feelings of awe."

The psychology of these words would seem transparent. But Russell's unconscious desire to be reunited with his parents does not explain *away* his passionate involvement in mathematics. From his earliest years he exhibited an exceptional clarity of thought which was ideally suited to mathematics. Yet this clarity often masked near-impenetrable complexities, and not only in mathematics. Russell would always feel the need to give clear and candid expression to his thoughts, yet things would seldom be as clear-cut as he wished them to appear. His solitary cogitations soon led him to reject any woolly notion of God, especially the personal God so beloved by his grandmother. Throughout his life Russell would profess, with rational and persuasive clarity, his atheistic belief—his "vain search for God"—yet at the same time retain an attitude toward mathematics that he expressed in terms of mystic religiosity. He *believed* in the abstract world of mathematics and was driven to search in it for the certainty that had, during his early childhood, vanished from his life.

At sixteen Russell was sent to a London crammer, where he was a boarder for almost two years. The pupils were mainly being crammed for the army exams, and Russell found them a decidedly coarse and ignorant lot. This accurate assessment of most potential army officers would unfortunately color Russell's entire view of humanity to the end of his days. Despite his much-avowed concern for the plight of his fellow beings, Russell would always find it difficult to disguise a certain aristocratic aloofness. This would intensify into disdain when he found himself confronted by those who chose to devote their lives to less noble pursuits, such as soldiers, statesmen, and authorities of any sort.

In 1890, at the age of eighteen, Russell won a scholarship to Trinity College, Cambridge, where Isaac Newton had studied and taught. For Russell's first three years he studied mathematics, which proved a bitter disappointment. For the most part, British mathematics had languished in the 150 years since Newton's day, and nowhere was this more apparent than at his alma mater. The celebrated "wrangler" examinations, designed to discover the finest mathematicians in Cambridge, required little more than formidable rote learning and ever more ingenious mathematical conjuring tricks. This was a mockery of the abstract beauty which had so inspired Russell, and in his fourth year he turned in disgust to philosophy.

Here he discovered the abstract world to end all abstract worlds, in the form of the all-embracing metaphysical system first conceived by the early-nineteenth-century German philosopher Hegel. A modern variant of Hegel's Absolute Idealism was taught at Cambridge by J. M. E. McTaggart. According to this, both time and matter were unreal. Only the Absolute Spirit, which contained everything, had reality. This ultimate reality was a whole, whose parts were all interrelated. Russell would liken this whole to a jelly: the moment you touched one part of it, the whole quivered. Yet unlike a jelly, this whole could not be cut up into *separate* parts. According to McTaggart, although this ultimate reality existed in an idealistic world above and beyond the so-called reality we experienced, it was still possible to deduce its nature. This could be done by starting from certain self-evident truths and just two empirical premises—namely, that something exists, and that it has parts. As is evident, this Absolute Idealism not only uncannily resembled the world of mathematics, it also went beyond it, subsuming the merely mathematical into the greater scheme of things in an overall philosophy. Russell was entranced. Here was a philosophy that fulfilled his twin needs—for the certainty of geometry and the mystical sublime.

But Russell also found that he possessed merely human needs. Even before he went to Cambridge he had met and fallen in love with an American Quaker called Alys Pearsall Smith. He was only seventeen, she was twenty-two—a five-year age difference which represented a yawning gap in their development. Russell did not declare his calf love, letting it mature in secret. Alys held advanced social views but remained strictly religious and devoted part of her time to delivering speeches at temperance rallies. Only four years later did Russell reveal his feelings, whereupon he was pleasantly surprised to find them reciprocated. In such an era of suppressed emotion, when so few had any experience of dealing with their feelings, even platonic love could quickly become a consuming passion. Within months Bertie and Alys were planning to be married. Lady Russell's reaction was predictable. Outraged that this American gold digger had corrupted her angelic Bertie, she did everything in her power to put an end to the romance. Bertie stood his ground—amidst the tears, railings, accusations of ingratitude, and threats—promising that he would marry Alys as soon as he was twenty-one. Then he would be legally free to make his own decisions and would also inherit an income sufficient to support them both. In 1894 they were married.

Russell had graduated with a first-class degree in moral science (philosophy) and was now elected a fellow of Trinity College. This appointment entailed no binding duties other than research. Mr. and Mrs. Russell set off on a tour of Europe, where they settled for an extended period in Germany. Here Russell developed an interest in politics and even wrote a book called *German Social Democracy*, which became his first published work.

When Russell finally returned to Cambridge he was introduced to G. E. Moore, who was widely regarded as the new young intellectual star of the university. Moore's attitude to philosophy was obstinately robust. He rejected McTaggart's idealism on the grounds that it simply defied common sense. Moore insisted on believing in the physical world he experienced. Russell's thinking had been undergoing a sea change, and he quickly established a rapport with Moore. Russell began to realize that the Hegelian world of Absolute Idealism bore no relation to the actualities of physical experience. But science and material reality simply could not be ignored. Russell found himself adopting an empirical materialist view of the world. Experience is what is real, and what we experience is the material world. Yet he found himself unable to relinquish his mystical belief in mathematics. "The greatest men who have been philosophers have felt the need of both science and mysticism." The need to reconcile these apparent disparities made philosophy "a greater thing than either science or religion." Russell now attempted to do just this, by embarking upon an investigation into the principles of mathematics. His thinking had come full circle. The twenty-six-year-old man was tackling the question raised by the eleven-year-old boy on his first encounter with Euclid. How could one discover the ultimate principles upon which mathematics was based? As Russell put it at the time: "Although the work is almost wholly mathematical, its interest is almost wholly philosophical." His search was for ultimate certainty.

Euclid had begun with axioms; these were the basis of geometry. But what was the basis of these axioms? They weren't just random—surely they had to conform to something? Russell concluded that this ultimate something could only be logic. The basic axioms of geometry, and likewise the fundamental concepts of mathematics as a whole, had to be logical. So what was the logical basis from which mathematics was derived?

In July 1900 Russell attended the International Congress of Philosophy in Paris. Here he met the Italian mathematical logician Giuseppe Peano, who had been working for several years upon the foundations of number. Peano's aim was to reach beyond the idea of number as simple intuition, and instead establish a logical method on which the concept of number could be founded, and from which the numbers themselves could be generated. In the course of this he had developed a series of fundamental logical symbols which enabled concepts and propositions to be analyzed into their ultimate constituent parts. For instance, he introduced separate symbols for "a class which has one member" and "the member of this class." This subtlety enabled him to overcome the previous logical confusion between the concepts "is a member of," "is contained in," and "is equal to." Russell was deeply impressed: he had never before encountered such precise logical rigor. He had been having extreme difficulty in his attempt to unravel the basic principles of mathematics. But now: "My sensations resembled those one has after climbing a mountain in a mist, when, on reaching the summit, the mist suddenly clears, and the country becomes visible for forty miles in every direction."

Previously Russell had seen the universe as a bowl of jelly; now he likened it to a bucket of shot. The whole had given way to a myriad of discrete parts. This required a diametrically different approach. Instead of synthesis, it was now necessary to apply analysis—which derives from the Greek word *to unravel*. The bucket of shot consisted of separate parts, each in contact only with those around it. Any understanding of this new discrete universe required an analysis of the relations between the separate parts.

The emphasis was now on the atomic nature of the universe, which was amenable to logical analysis. Here Russell was not so much referring to physical atoms as to the ancient Greek idea that gave rise to the notion of atoms. According to the fifth-century B.C. philosopher Democritus, if one went on dividing matter one must in the end come to something indivisible. This would be uncuttable—in Greek *a-tomos,* hence the word atom. Democritus had not reached this notion by experiment but purely by logical reasoning. This was now Russell's aim too. He wished to reach the indivisible atoms of logic on which mathematics was based. Initially he had arrived at the basic concept of "number," "order," and "whole and part." But Peano had shown him how to go beyond the immediate intuition of number, by demonstrating it could be generated from certain even more fundamental postulates:

1. 0 is a number.
2. The successor of any number is a number.
3. No two numbers have the same successor.
4. 0 is not the successor of any number.

Russell was not entirely persuaded by this logic, but he recognized at once that its method held the key. Instead of his previous concept of "whole and parts," he decided to use the notion of "class" (as in "the class of all apples," "the class of all unsolved problems," etc.). Class is a logical distinction: it is based upon the fundamental logical law of identity. A thing cannot at the same time be both itself and not itself. (The world is divided into "apples" and "things that are not apples.") Russell was able to show that the notion of class is prior to that of number. For example, we can conceive of the class of apples without collecting all apples and placing them together. Without counting the number of apples in this class, we can still say some very definite things about it. That is: This class will include no pears; its members will all be fruit; and so on. From this it could be seen that the notion of class is logically prior to that of number. In other words, the logical notion of class was more fundamental than that of number.

Russell then proceeded to use the notion of class to generate the concept of number, and then all the individual numbers. A simplified version of Russell's method goes as follows:

—The class of all objects that are not identical to themselves has 0 members.

—But all empty classes have the same members, so they are not equal to one another; they are in fact identical. They are the *same* class.

—There is thus just one empty class. Hence from 0 we have generated the notion of 1.

—The class of empty classes thus contains one member. So the class of empty classes and its member make 2. And the class of the class of empty classes and its member lead us to generate the number 3, and so forth.

—The whole of mathematics could be generated out of the logical notion of classes, which derived from the fundamental logical notion of identity.

With this method Russell had established two vital points. He had shown that the truths of mathematics could be translated into the truths of logic. And this showed that mathematics in fact had no distinct subject matter of its own, such as numbers. All mathematical truths were thus in theory ultimately reducible to logical form. This meant that they could be *proved* by logic. (The wish of the eleven-year-old child had come true: even the axioms of geometry could be proved!)

In 1903, Russell published *The Principles of Mathematics*. This work established him as a major philosophical thinker, especially in Europe where this topic had become a matter of intense speculation. With the new century, philosophy was moving away from the grandiose specula-tions of metaphysics, epitomized by Hegel, and had begun to concentrate on the more precise problem of human knowledge. What was the basis of our knowledge, and how could we know if it was true? The first step had been to apply this question to the most certain and infal-lible knowledge available, namely mathematics. And the answer appeared to lie in logical analy-sis. It was generally agreed that Russell had not answered the question completely; there was still the problem of less rigid forms of knowledge such as science. But thinkers recognized that Russell had made a significant step toward answering one of the problems that had troubled philosophers since ancient Greek times.

Since Russell's point was essentially philosophical, *The Principles of Mathematics* had been written in plain English (or as near to that mythical entity as philosophers can come). But as Peano had shown, language can frequently gloss over crucial logical distinctions. Russell now intended to write a second volume which would set down his argument in the more precise form of logical symbols, thus overcoming possible misinterpretations. The immense difficulties arising from this project led him to collaborate with the Cambridge mathematician Alfred North Whitehead, who had taught Russell during his undergraduate days. Whitehead was the only mathematician at Cambridge whom Russell admired; Whitehead also had a thorough knowledge of philosophy and logic. This would be an equal partnership. Together the two of them set about developing a symbolic logic which extended Peano's original conception. This was the beginning of *Principia Mathematica,* a collaboration that would eventually take Russell and Whitehead no less than ten years. In Russell's words, they would show that "logic is the youth of mathematics and mathematics is the manhood of logic." They would start with an irreducible minimum of logical concepts, represented in clear symbolic form. They would then advance, step by logical step, to show how the whole of logic, and then mathematics, could be derived from these basic concepts alone. This would be an immense project, often requiring fiendish ingenuity, involving many hundreds of pages covered with logical symbols. But it would be worth it. What it would establish would be absolute and irrefutable: the status of human knowledge would be transformed forever. This would be the greatest advance in philosophic certainty since Aristotle's initial discovery of logic more than two millennia earlier.

Three years into this project, disaster struck. Russell discovered a flaw which ran to the heart of their logical argument. This was a paradox which seemed to render the very notion of classes self-contradictory. Today it is known as Russell's Paradox.

Imagine a library, which besides its shelves of books also includes two catalogs. The first catalog lists all books that refer to themselves—for example, "as mentioned previously in Chapter 2." The second catalog lists all books in the library that do not refer to themselves. In which catalog is the second catalog listed? If it is listed in itself, it immediately becomes a book that does refer to itself. But it cannot be listed in the first catalog because it does not refer to itself. The paradox appears irreducible.

But what has this got to do with classes? In Russell's form, the argument runs as follows: Instead of the two catalogs, we have two classes. First there is the class of all classes that are members of themselves. For instance, the class of all classes *is* a member of itself, because it is itself a class. Second, we have the class of all classes that are not members of themselves. Among these is the class of all numbers, which is not itself a number. Now, is the class of all classes that are not members of themselves a member of itself? If it is, it is not. If it is not, it is. The same paradox as the library catalog ensues.

This may appear trivial, which it did at first to Russell. But the trouble is, it destroys the entire notion of class as a logical entity. And it was from classes that number was generated. Without the notion of classes, it was impossible to progress from logic to mathematics in a logically irrefutable manner. Mathematics could not be reduced to logic after all. It was not logically necessary, it was contingent. Its procedures *within* itself may have been rigidly logical, but as a system it was ultimately based upon axioms that had no logical justification. In a sense these axioms were arbitrary, there was no *reason* for them. These were axioms you just had to accept without further justification, like the eleven-year-old boy being taught Euclid by his elder brother.

The more Russell pondered this paradox, the more profound and insurmountable it appeared to become. He wrote of his discovery to the great German mathematical logician Gottlob Frege, who for many years had been engaged upon a similar project. Frege was thunderstruck, his life's work seemingly in ruins. In his reply to Russell he exclaimed: "Arithmetic is finished!" Russell struggled on: "Every morning I would sit down before a blank sheet of paper. Throughout the day, with a brief interval for lunch, I would stare at the blank sheet. Often when evening came it was still empty." Russell wrote to the great French mathematician Henri Poincaré, who replied that Russell's Paradox was little more than a version of the ancient Greek paradox posed by Epimenedes the Cretan when he stated: "All Cretans are liars." Russell wrote down on a piece of paper: "'All Cretans are liars,' said the Cretan," and stared at this for days on end. One of the finest philosophical minds in Europe, at the height of his powers, was reduced to pondering what appeared to be no more than a birthday-party puzzle. His mind remained balked, day after day. And as if this weren't enough: "I made a practice of wandering about the common every night from eleven till one, by which means I came to know the three different noises made by night jars. (Most people only know one.) I was trying hard to solve the contradictions mentioned above."

Finally, in 1906, Russell came up with an answer in the form of his Theory of Types. This distinguished a hierarchy of ascending classes, or *types* of classes. Thus there was a class of cats and a higher class of animals. What was true for one type of class was not necessarily true for the type above it. What was true for classes of individuals (e.g., cats) would not always hold true for classes of classes (e.g., animals). A class could be a member of itself (e.g., the class of all classes), but it could not refer to itself. Self-referring classes were without meaning. For instance, to speak of "the class of all cats that are feline" was nonsensical. This became even more evident in speaking of "the class of all cats that are not feline." As Russell put it: "Whatever involves all of a collection must not be one of a collection." This meant that neither the "class of all classes that are members of themselves" nor the "class of all classes that are not members of themselves" could contain itself. The paradox was resolved!

Russell was overjoyed, and declared, "After this it only remained to write the book out." Even so, finishing *Principia Mathematica* proved no easy task. Whitehead could no longer assist Russell, owing to his teaching duties at Cambridge. In order to complete their collaboration, Russell found himself working ten to twelve hours a day for the next eight months. When finally completed, *Principia Mathematica* consisted of three volumes extending over four thousand pages of rigorous, meticulously argued symbolic logic. Each step had to be argued from fundamentals—to such an extent that the proposition "1 + 1 = 2" was not reached until the middle of volume two!

Not surprisingly, Russell later declared: "My intellect never quite recovered from the strain." Russell had finished *Principia Mathematica* by 1909, but publication of the three volumes continued over the next three years. Such a work was scarcely expected to become a best-seller, but even for philosophers and mathematicians it proved formidably abstruse. Russell later declared that he knew of only six people who had managed to read all three volumes. Despite this, *Principia Mathematica* was greeted as "an epoch in the history of speculative thought." In time it would have profound influence on mathematical, scientific, and philosophic investigation throughout Europe.

Russell's Theory of Types paved the way for logical positivism, the predominant European philosophy of the 1920s and 1930s. His discovery that a proposition could be syntactically and logically correct yet at the same time meaningless was seminal to logical positivist thought. For the logical positivists, the meaning of a proposition consisted in the method of its verification. This led them to distinguish three types of propositions.

Propositions involving mathematics and logic were judged to be tautological. That is, one part of the proposition was in the end an explication of the other. (For example: $2 + 2 = 4$, or even $x^n + y^n = z^n$.)

The second type of proposition could be verified by experience. This would include all statements such as "Today is Thursday." It would also include all scientific statements; for example, "Water boils at 100 degrees centigrade." All such statements had a means of verification.

The third type of proposition contained metaphysical statements such as "God exists" or "The universe has a purpose." Since such propositions were unverifiable, it was pointless to talk about them. Statements of this kind were meaningless.

But this led to two snags. All ethical and historical statements fell into the third category. Strictly speaking, statements such as "Eating people is wrong" and "Columbus sailed across the Atlantic in 1492" remained unverifiable. A third objection proved even more damning. The statement "the meaning of a proposition is its method of verification" also fell into the third category. This paradox, unlike Russell's, refused to go away.

But even Russell's Paradox proved not to be permanently banished. It was soon discovered that not all self-referring classes were nonsensical or meaningless. Indeed, several well-established categories of mathematics relied upon self-referring classes. These could not be abandoned; on the other hand, there appeared to be no logical way of distinguishing them from nonsensical classes. The attempt to prove that mathematics is logical was now leading into even murkier waters. This latest development seemed to hint that mathematics itself might contain paradoxes that lay beyond the reach of logic. This was, of course, totally unacceptable. Yet all attempts to prove otherwise came to naught. This state of affairs was not to be finally resolved until 1931. Then, to the horror of all concerned, the twenty-five-year-old Austrian Kurt Gödel succeeded in showing that mathematics *did* contain a paradox. Gödel produced a logical proof which demonstrated this once and for all. According to Gödel's proof, any complex system, such as mathematics, that attempted to base itself upon axioms was bound to contain within it certain apparently true propositions that could not be proved, or disproved, within that system. One always had to introduce a further axiom, outside the system, in order to prove or disprove such propositions. Yet as soon as any new axiom was introduced that rendered such propositions provable, this only generated further propositions that could neither be proved nor disproved. In other words, any attempt to base mathematics upon a set of basic axioms was doomed from the outset. Mathematics was by its very nature "incomplete." This left the philosophers and logicians in a quandary. Yet mathematics did not grind to a halt, and mathematicians blithely persisted in their illogical pursuit. The situation remains unresolved to this day, and mathematicians continue to believe in mathematics regardless of Gödel's damning indictment. They adopt the commonsense view that while there may be no (philosophical) reason to believe in mathematics, they will continue illogically to do so—because it works. The bridges built according to mathematical specifications don't collapse, the airplanes don't fall out of the sky, even the rockets manage to land on Mars. There are times when theory may have good reason, but practice has better ones.

The years spent writing *Principia Mathematics* had climaxed in Russell's eight months of solitary agonizing mental effort. Yet the previous years had not been uneventful. This was largely due to Russell's emotional immaturity. Given the times and his upbringing, this handicap is perhaps understandable. Where the emotions of others were concerned, he was capable of easygoing flippancy with his college pals, yet where his own emotions were concerned, he remained intense and willful. Emotional questions were subjected to an unswerving and inappropriate intellectual scrutiny. Russell was a man of deep principle *and* a philosopher (not always the same thing). When his intellectual reasoning led him to the realization of a truth, he believed in disclosing this truth—and, when necessary, acting upon it. The most notorious example of this took place in 1903. "I went out bicycling one afternoon, and suddenly, as I was riding along a country road, I realized that I no longer loved Alys. I had no idea until this moment that my love for her was even lessening." Was Russell's emotional maturity really so undeveloped that he could only understand his feelings in such spontaneous "realizations"? Or was this just a self-serving fib? Like the philosophical paradox named after him (which Russell was pondering deeply during this period), it was evidently both and yet neither.

Russell felt it was his moral duty to inform Alys of what he had realized. The effect was predictably devastating. Yet one can't help thinking that Alys—an older and somewhat more self-aware human being—must surely have perceived that all was not well between them. As it was, she refused to accept Russell's inspired flash of self-knowledge and clung to him. Russell found this irksome. The intransigent behavior of both partners meant that for the next eight years their marriage sank deeper and deeper into misery. Despite spells apart, they would not finally separate until 1911. During this time both would suffer from occasional bouts of almost total despair—Russell's would sometimes be intellectual as well as emotional. When the difficulties of his immense philosophical labor overwhelmed him, he would walk in the woods at night con-

templating suicide. Alys's misery back in the
bedroom can only be imagined.

This was a highly emotional decade for Russell as he fell rapidly in love, and bicycled
equally rapidly out of love, with a succession of
women. These affairs were intense, occasionally
one-sided, occasionally platonic, occasionally
with unhappily married women. They appear to
have involved the few women who showed any
interest in this somewhat odd-looking little aristocratic figure with a ragged mustache and bird-
like mannerisms. At one stage he even fell in love
with the invalid wife of his collaborator and
close friend Whitehead. Russell suffered considerable guilt over these affairs, for despite being
an emotional loose cannon he remained a man
of principle and at heart even something of a puritan. He was finally cured of these afflictions in
1910, when at the age of thirty-eight he fell in
love with Lady Ottoline Morrell, the exotic
thirty-seven-year-old wife of an amiably com-
plaisant member of Parliament and brewery
owner.

Ottoline was renowned for her shock of marmalade-colored hair, her heavily powdered horselike face, and her exotic, brightly colored outfits. She was by turns domineering, insouciant, and desperately unsure of herself. This combination appears to have made her an intriguing and highly attractive personality. And not just to Russell. The Bloomsbury Group would later enjoy regular weekends at Garsington, the Morrells' country house in Oxfordshire—though they never really accepted Ottoline and were characteristically catty about her behind her back. Even more so when she was seen to have captivated such an intellectual giant as Russell.

During the course of their five-year affair, she and Russell corresponded regularly. As far as he could, Russell opened both his heart and his mind to her. She, in her way, "humanized" him. It was Ottoline, in her extravagant normality, who showed Russell how it was possible for him too to live a normal life. In their own flawed ways, as best they could, they came to love each other.

But this was not the most intense of Russell's

affairs during these years. Predictably, his major encounter was an affair of the mind. Less predictably, it was Russell who played the more mature role in this passionate, combative, but nonsexual relationship. Ludwig Wittgenstein turned up unannounced at Russell's Cambridge rooms one October afternoon in 1911. He was strikingly handsome, with a stiff Viennese manner. From the outset he insisted upon speaking in halting English, despite the fact that Russell spoke fluent German. Wittgenstein was a scion of the most powerful industrial family in the Austro-Hungarian Empire. Initially he had been educated privately in the family palace, where Brahms would sometimes be hired to give private recitals. Later he studied engineering at Berlin and then aeronautics at Manchester, where he became interested in the foundations of mathematics. Typically, he demanded to know who were the leading figures in this field, and was told of Russell and Frege. Without further ado the inexperienced young engineering student set off to discuss his first logical ideas on the foundations of mathematics with the two world authorities in this field. As Wittgenstein put it, the irritated Frege "wiped the floor" with him. Russell, on the other hand, was intrigued. He recognized at once that there was something exceptional about Wittgenstein. Consciously or unconsciously, he may even have recognized his younger self. Wittgenstein believed passionately in his philosophical quest: it had become his entire life. When he appeared to fall short of his high ideals, his first thought was of suicide.

Wittgenstein quickly became a regular unannounced visitor to Russell's rooms. He would drop in around midnight, pace agitatedly up and down the carpet without saying a word, then interrogate Russell earnestly. Should he commit suicide? Should he become a philosopher, or should he become an aeronaut? Russell advised against suicide or becoming an aeronaut (two not dissimilar activities in those days). Wittgenstein decided that he would become a philosopher after all, and began bombarding Russell with his ideas on logic. Russell guided him patiently, arguing perceptively, opening Wittgenstein's mind to the philosophical problems involved. Owing to Wittgenstein's "fire and penetration and intellectual purity," within a matter of months he was grappling with fundamental problems. Wittgenstein, who at twenty-two was just over half Russell's age, was arrogant, persistent, and unbending. For him, logic was the holy grail. Russell, who had just spent ten years understanding the deepest problems and limitations of logic, was gently insistent.

In the course of one celebrated argument, Russell asked Wittgenstein to consider the proposition: "There is no hippopotamus in this room at present." Wittgenstein refused to accept the truth of this proposition, on the grounds that it was not logically necessary. Russell immediately began looking under the desks, wondering aloud where the hippopotamus could possibly be. But Wittgenstein still refused to believe in Russell's proposition. It was *logically* possible that a hippopotamus was in the room. Russell insisted that it could not be so, on empirical grounds. Here lay the seeds of their future divergence. Wittgenstein would base his philosophy upon logic and language. Russell's philosophy was more concerned with scientific reality.

After analyzing the foundations of mathematics in *Principia Mathematica,* Russell extended his investigation to epistemology in general—that is, to the grounding of all knowledge. What is the connection—if any—between "our" knowledge and the "external world"? Russell began by examining our experience. Evidently it was possible to be deceived by what we experience—in dreams, mirages, delusions, and so forth. On the other hand, it was simply not plausible to doubt the whole of our experience on this basis. He believed that "you should set to work to doubt things and retain only what you cannot doubt because of its clearness and distinctness." This clearness and distinctness arises from the basics of our experience: "sense data." These sense data are the individual perceptions we receive through our sight, hearing, smell, taste, and touch. Such entities are not purely mental, yet they are not in themselves the material objects which act on our senses. We can speak of ordinary objects—such as an apple—but our acquaintance with such an object is made up of individual sense data. These are what give us the sensation red, round, solid, smooth, and so forth, which lead us to construct the object "apple." Likewise the coherence, consistence, and continuance of the world of objects. The continuing objects of the material world consist of *logical constructions* out of our sense data.

From this theory of epistemology it is easy to progress to the scientific worldview. All instruments of measurement and observation are but extensions of our senses. These too provide us with nothing more or less than sense data. From the faintest pinpoint of twinkling light observed through a telescope, we logically construct a vast star millions of light years away. By passing light through a spectrometer we can logically construct the minuscule wavelength of that light.

One hundred fifty years earlier, the Scottish philosopher David Hume had outlined the ultimate empirical theory of epistemology. All certain human knowledge was based upon the impressions on our "sensations, passions, and motions." Our knowledge of the outside world came from perception alone—even our understanding of such things as bodies, causality, and so forth was reached only by the uncertain process of induction. We did not *know* that a billiard ball was an individual object. This was simply an interpretation of our impressions, an induced idea. We did not *know* that the sun would rise tomorrow morning, or that flame burns paper—such knowledge was mere assumption based upon our induced idea of probability or causation. Is Russell in fact saying anything more than this? The key to Russell's theory of knowledge, and its originality, lies in his emphasis upon logical construction. We do not actually experience an enduring material object such as a "mountain." This notion is assembled by a process of logical construction which only begins with our sense data.

Russell's aim was nothing less than to reunite philosophy and science, as had been the case in ancient Greece and again in the seventeenth century. (Newton's great work on gravity was called

Mathematical Principles of Natural Philosophy.)
But here Russell came up against a difficulty. If I
simply constructed the material world out of
sense data, what then was the material world itself? Was it simply a logical construction inside
my head? Did it have no independent existence
outside my mental processes, outside my head?
And if it did, how could I know about it?

Russell now turned to the problem of the
external world. Previously he had worked "for-
ward" from sense data—with the logical construction of knowledge. Now he worked
"backward" from sense data to construct matter.
The stuff of the world, matter itself, consisted of
"all the sense data which all possible observers
could observe in perceiving the same thing." A
material object viewed and perceived from all
possible perspectives *was* that material object.
The sense data were functions of the object.

Matter was not some mysterious unknow-
able secret lurking behind our perceptions of it,
as previous philosophers such as Kant had sug-
gested. There was no enigma, no secret about the
world—just "science and sober daylight and the

business of the day." Philosophy, and the world, were as clear and obvious as science would have them. Sense data were a direct relation between the mind and the nonmental world—whether they were physical objects or abstract ideas. The latter category gave a platonic reality to such things as our idea of beauty or goodness as well as such entities as number. These "existed" in abstract form. In this way the mind was directly related to mathematics too. So concepts such as number were analagous to basic sense data.

Our mental processes dealt with these basic notions—color, number, and so forth—as atomic "simples." In the same way that the world was made of atoms and combinations of atoms, our knowledge was constructed of these atomic simples. These could be manipulated, combined, or classified—by the use of logic. This led Russell to call his philosophy "logical atomism." In order to discover whether a statement was true, we could break it down into its logical atoms and see whether these had been combined in a correct logical fashion. This method came to be known as logical analysis, and it became one of the dominant forces in twentieth-century philosophy.

A simple example of logical analysis can be used on the following proposition: "The present king of France is bald." This appears to state a simple relation, which can be either true or false. But in reality it presents us with a paradox. It is neither true nor false—it is nonsensical. Why? Because there is no such thing as "the present king of France." This proposition can be analyzed into constituent atomic parts: "present existence," "the king of France," and "being bald." Quite plainly, the original proposition should in fact read: "There exists such a thing as the king of France, and he is bald." The first part of this is false, and consequently "the king of France" cannot stand in relation to "being bald."

While he worked on these problems, Russell tried out many of his developing ideas on Wittgenstein. They were soon working as equals. Yet beneath this apparent philosophical partnership, deep divergences were beginning to appear. Wittgenstein insisted upon the primacy of logic while Russell's epistemology was becoming increasingly concerned with the notion of matter, the "real world" of science. This was a particularly exciting period of scientific discovery—one of the greatest in scientific history. Einstein had published his first paper of special relativity in 1905. According to this, time and motion were relative, and matter was a form of energy ($E = mc^2$). Meanwhile, by 1912 Niels Bohr was beginning to develop quantum theory, which showed that the laws of classical physics no longer held true at subatomic levels. Space and time were not absolute; illogically light could be both a solid particle and a wave (which has no mass). Russell was aware of these developments. Clearly any new philosophical theory of knowledge would have to take account of such revolutionary developments. In the light of relativity and quantum theory, epistemology as it was then understood simply fell apart.

Many still question whether it has recovered. Einstein and Bohr were both highly intrigued by the epistemological problems posed by their discoveries. Nowadays scientists dealing with ultimate subatomic entities such as quarks and superstrings are no longer interested in epistemology. Are superstrings real particles or simply mathematical entities? Such questions are a matter of indifference to them. Superstrings "work" in their equations: this is all that matters to the scientists. They react to the illogicality of science much as mathematicians did to Gödel's disproof of mathematical certainty. So does philosophy still have something to say about matter, or is epistemology to all intents and purposes redundant here?

Russell recognized the fundamental importance of this issue and was determined to address it. Wittgenstein, on the other hand, saw the foundations of epistemology as lying elsewhere. Both Russell and Wittgenstein placed great emphasis on logic, but beyond this their philosophical paths were to part. For Russell, there was more to philosophy than logic. For Wittgenstein, logic was supreme. He agreed with Russell about the atomic constituents of knowledge and the need to analyze language in order to arrive at these constituents. But for Wittgenstein the structure of language revealed the structure of the world. His first great work, *Tractatus Logico-Philosophicus,* stated quite plainly: "The world is the totality of facts, not of things. . . . The facts in logical space are the world." From this starting point, he would eventually conclude: "Of that which we cannot speak, we must remain silent." In other words, knowledge must speak logically or not at all.

Fortunately, scientists investigating the ultimate constituents of matter—and their illogical behavior—did not cop out in this fashion. And in not so doing they gave the lie to Wittgenstein's admonition. Language *can* deal with the illogical. It can also deal with a reality beyond that of logic itself: nuclear physics achieved supreme advances during the twentieth century. Wittgenstein's avoidance of such issues and his withdrawal into a world of logic meant that philosophy could continue to operate with considerable success in cut-and-dried certainty. Hence his dominant position in twentieth-century philosophy. By contrast, Russell's philosophy never satisfactorily solved the more comprehensive range of problems it addressed. Russell's continuing attempt to solve these problems gave his philosophy an increasingly makeshift appearance. Compared with the clear but complex certainties of Wittgenstein, Russell's brave and comprehensive attempt appeared as mere confusion.

Even so, Russell learned a great deal from Wittgenstein. He later characterized getting to know Wittgenstein as the most exciting experience of his intellectual life. But he was eventually dazzled by the complexities that Wittgenstein discussed, his confidence undermined by the almost insane passion of Wittgenstein's onslaughts on his philosophical position. This eventually led Russell to conclude that philosophy had become too difficult for him now that he had reached his early forties. He convinced himself that he would never again be capable of original work. In this philosophical battle of wills between two giants, there was no doubting who had won. How much this was due to force of personality rather than relevance of philosophical argument is open to question.

Despite this setback, Russell was far from being a broken man. If anything, it was only now that his deeper human qualities began to emerge. Having abandoned the attempt to forge a comprehensive original philosophy, he now took to writing popular philosophy. In a series of deceptively simple books, which he continued writing regularly throughout the rest of his long life, he addressed everything from specific ethical problems to the entire history of Western philosophy. The first of these books was completed in 1912 and called *The Problems of Philosophy*. For many people this remains the quintessential introduction to the subject. Wittgenstein was horrified that Russell should now sink so low as to introduce people of lesser genius than himself to philosophy. From now on he treated his former mentor with patronizing contempt. Despite this, Russell later generously assisted Wittgenstein at two crucial junctures of his life—ensuring that his *Tractatus Logico-Philosophicus* was published, and that he was able to obtain a post at Cambridge during the 1930s despite his total lack of academic qualifications.

Russell's philosophical interests had always extended beyond the claustrophobic limits of logic. Political, ethical, and aesthetic questions had persistently interested him. And not just in theory. His outlook was liberal, and he joined in the political and ethical debates of the day with some vigor. The most contentious social issue in Britain during the years preceding World War I was the woman suffrage movement, led by Emmeline Pankhurst, who was jailed several times for her protests. At a time when the expression of such views often led to social ostracism, Russell was all in favor of giving women the vote. In 1907 he even stood for Parliament at the Wimbledon by-election, campaigning for woman suffrage and free trade. This caused a nationwide furor, with Russell receiving many more insults than votes. (Women would not get the vote in Britain until 1918, two years before the United States.) Despite this setback, Russell continued to play an active role in politics, campaigning for the Liberal party during elections—which was how he first met Lady Ottoline Morrell, whose husband was a Liberal member of Parliament.

In a reversal of the usual process, Russell's principles appeared to become more radical the older he became. At the turn of the century he had allowed himself to be carried along on the tide of imperialistic patriotism that accompanied the Boer War, when the British army defeated the Dutch settlers in southern Africa. By 1914, when World War I broke out, he was forty-two and had rationalized his liberal principles. He had decided that war was wrong, and led a number of highly unpopular pacifist protests in London. This led to him being expelled from his lecturing post at Trinity College, Cambridge.

But Russell was not one to be dissuaded from his principles by being thrown out of a job. He persisted. In 1918 he was sentenced to six months in Brixton Prison—a spell of solitude which he welcomed, for it freed him from distraction and enabled him to return to serious philosophical writing. The end result was *Analysis of Mind,* where he came to the important conclusion that the difference between mind and matter was illusory. Matter was more mental, and mind more material, than commonly supposed. This approach attempted to overcome the difficulty of sense data. These may have been a "function" of matter, but they had also been regarded as "atomic simples" in the mind—an impossibility as long as there was a distinction between mind and matter. Mind was now viewed not as some kind of thinking substance that received data, but as somehow made up of these sense data and "simples" (such as abstract ideas, number, etc.). What had previously been conceived of as mind was constructed out of what had previously been conceived of as matter and other platonic entities external to it.

Ottoline had been highly supportive of Russell during his anti-war campaign, but the passion in their affair now dwindled to the point where they were simply close friends. Russell's liberal principles had long led him to advocate free love, but it was only now that he began to practice it. (His previous bout of promiscuity, after falling out of love with Alys, appears to have been a succession of spontaneous infatuations arising from emotional incontinence, regardless of any moral outlook.) He had a number of affairs, most notably with the twenty-one-year-old actress Colette O'Niel, the writer Katherine Mansfield, and Vivien Eliot, the mentally unstable first wife of the poet T. S. Eliot.

But in 1919 he met Dora Black, an independent-minded, pipe-smoking twenty-five-year-old who had gained a first-class degree in modern languages at Cambridge. Dora had admired Russell's pacifist stance but likened him personally to the Mad Hatter from *Alice in Wonderland* (a perceptive assessment that had struck more than one acquaintance). She and Russell held intense conversations in which they both declared their profound disbelief in marriage. Dora was a radical feminist who declared that her aim in life was to have children. These would be brought up entirely by their mother, there being no place for a father in such matters. "Well, whoever I have children with, it won't be you," replied Russell.

It was perhaps inevitable that they would marry, but this did not happen for two years. During this period they remained together, and both traveled to see the new Bolshevik Russia. When the Revolution had broken out in 1917 it had inspired Russell to believe that at last a just society might be established somewhere on earth. He departed for Russia with high hopes, as a member of a Labour party delegation— most of whose delegates regarded themselves as pilgrims going to witness the new era. In recognition of his philosophic eminence, Russell was granted a private audience with Lenin. The British philosopher was unimpressed by the leader of the Revolution and horrified by what he saw of its effects, especially among the starving peasants in the countryside. Dora, who traveled on a different itinerary and saw Lenin address a crowded meeting, returned ecstatic.

Immediately after his trip Russell wrote *The Theory and Practice of Bolshevism,* which criticized what he had seen and made him highly unpopular in left-wing British circles. Most visitors were taken in by what they saw—or imagined they saw. H. G. Wells, who visited Russia the same year, returned to write a series of enthusiastic articles in the *Sunday Express.* George Bernard Shaw, who traveled to Russia at the height of the 1930s purges, would compare

Stalin to the pope and Russia to a "splendid, sunny dream."

Russell always remained a radical, but he insisted upon telling the truth as he saw it. As a result, he retained few political friends through his long life. But his fiery arguments with Dora Black over Bolshevik Russia brought them closer together, and they were married in September 1921. Six days later Dora gave birth to Russell's first child, a son whom they called Conrad (after the great Polish novelist).

Dora felt that getting married was a serious betrayal of her principles. Russell was more equivocal. He feared that illegitimacy—a major social stigma in those days—might cause Conrad to resent his parents. With uncharacteristic pragmatism, he recognized that remaining unmarried, with an illegitimate son, would make it even more difficult to find academic work. His pacifist stance and his jail sentence made Russell persona non grata in British academic circles. Fortunately his international eminence brought him the occasional remunerative lecture tour in America—but not accompanied by a lover and illegitimate child. In order to earn sufficient income, Russell continued to write popular books on philosophy and issues of the day. He and Dora also wrote regular articles for the newspapers until Dora produced a second child, this time a daughter named Katherine.

There now arose the problem of the children's education. Being intellectuals with advanced principles, both the Russells were naturally against all forms of conventional education. So they decided the only thing to do was to open their own school, advertising for pupils from like-minded parents. Beacon Hill School, set amidst the Surrey countryside near Petersfield, opened in September 1927. Its prospectus described how the boarding pupils would be brought up as if they were members of a large, old-fashioned family. Lessons would not be compulsory, and the young pupils would be free to roam at large on the grounds. Instead of discipline, they would be encouraged to discuss their problems at the school council, a forum in which members of the staff were usually outnumbered, and outvoted, by other pupils. What the school council decided would then be implemented—except on one notable occasion, after a unanimous vote against prunes on the school menu. Dora vetoed this action on the grounds that prunes were essential to health.

The result of such a regime was perhaps inevitable. The children enjoyed themselves, as indeed did the staff. There is a photograph of a besuited Russell sitting on some steps with a child on his knee, surrounded by a group of somewhat ragged but undeniably happy children. The benign smile on Russell's face is probably the happiest picture we have of him. (One cannot help but ponder the psychology of this.) Alas, little in the way of academic learning seems to have taken place; and as time went by the children became increasingly rowdy. In mitigation it must be said that the school quickly became a dumping ground for unmanageable children, spoiled brats of rich parents, and those who simply didn't fit, most of whom had been expelled from other schools. These difficult and often damaged three- to twelve-year-olds probably benefited from the attentions of the determinedly free-thinking Russells. Yet arguing about the merits of prunes with eight-year-olds would scarcely seem the most productive activity for one of the world's leading philosophers. For there is no denying that this is what Russell remained (a philosopher, that is, rather than an eight-year-old).

Around this time Wittgenstein sent a manuscript of his work in progress to Trinity College, Cambridge, in the hope that they would employ him. This was immediately dispatched to Russell, who was considered the only philosopher competent to judge its merits. Although Wittgenstein had recently described Russell's work as "vomitive," Russell agreed to the thankless and exacting task of attempting to understand Wittgenstein's almost incomprehensible manuscript. Russell found himself deeply out of sympathy with the direction that his former pupil's philosophy had taken, yet he graciously acknowledged that Wittgenstein's new work was "very original, and indubitably important." This opinion proved crucial, and Wittgenstein was accepted. No letter of thanks reached Beacon Hill.

In 1931 Russell's elder brother Frank died, and he succeeded to the family title, becoming the 3rd Earl Russell. Frank had run through what remained of the family fortune, which meant that apart from the title, all Russell inherited were his brother's debts—which included four hundred pounds a year toward the upkeep of one of Frank's two divorced wives. Four years later the new Lord Russell emulated his predecessor by also obtaining a second divorced wife. His marriage to Dora had from the start been a matter of lofty liberal principle, accompanied by somewhat less lofty behavior. In the end Russell found that he was unable to maintain this elevated attitude after Lady Russell had one child, and then another, by her young American lover. A year later, in a triumph of optimism over experience, the sixty-three-year-old Russell married his twenty-five-year-old research assistant, who had copper-colored hair like Ottoline and smoked a pipe like Dora.

Two years later Russell moved to the United States, where a sequence of academic appointments was eventually terminated owing to Russell's public pronouncements on such matters as birth control and free love. During this period sex still didn't exist in Britain, and many states in America were even more vehement on the topic. When World War II broke out in Europe in 1939, Russell found himself stranded and broke in the United States. Living on hospitality from American friends, he settled down to write *A History of Western Philosophy,* which eventually ran to more than eight hundred pages. This entertaining, opinionated, and witty work saved him financially when it became a best-seller. It remains in print to this day as the finest one-volume work on the subject. As a result, it is constantly vilified by professional philosophers (many of whom would be out of a job had not this work originally inspired their students to study the subject).

In 1944 Russell returned to Britain where he was reappointed as a fellow of Trinity College, Cambridge. All was forgiven: he was now seventy-two years old and regarded as a national sage. His so-called popular books now became increasingly popular in actuality, amidst the liberalized climate of postwar Britain. He also gave regular talks on the radio. In those early days, before the concept of broadcasting was fully understood, distinguished speakers were occasionally allowed more than five minutes without interruption by advertising jingle, canned laughter, or jocular host, permitting Russell to elaborate on his ideas in comprehensible form. In 1950 he was awarded the Nobel Prize, ostensibly for literature but in fact more as "an apostle of humanity and free speech" (in the words of the BBC).

Although Russell enjoyed adulation—whether from a single person in love, or from the general public—his psychology did not allow him to tolerate such popularity for long. He soon found an opportunity to remedy this situation. The world was moving into the most frigid period of the cold war, and in 1954 Russell signed a joint manifesto with Einstein warning of the nuclear consequences of a third world war, which at the time seemed imminent. Two years later a conference attended by many of the world's leading physicists took placer at Pugwash, Nova Scotia, where they urged world leaders to avoid a nuclear war. Russell had been one of the prime movers behind this conference, but at eighty-four he was too frail to attend. Despite this, a year later he launched the Campaign for Nuclear Disarmament in Britain. True to form, as he became older his militancy grew. In 1960, following the example of Ghandi, he launched a campaign of civil disobedience against nuclear weapons. A year later he was arrested at a sit-down protest in Trafalgar Square in London. After an interval of forty-three years, he returned for a brief spell to Brixton Prison.

As Russell entered his nineties he became even more intransigent. During the late 1960s he became a leading international opponent of the American presence in Vietnam, taking part in protests and peace conferences. Between times he wrote his remarkably candid and lucid three-volume *Autobiography* (though he did gloss over a few episodes, as later biographers would point out with glee). As he approached the end of his long life, he still adhered to the three principles which had driven him through the years:

"the longing for love, the search for knowledge, and unbearable pity for the sufferings of mankind." Bertrand Russell died in 1970 at the age of ninety-seven.

Criticisms and Comments

Mathematics may be defined as the subject in which we never know what we are talking about, nor whether what we are saying is true.

—Russell, commenting on mathematics

Russell's curiosity and hope that it would lead to firm knowledge (the equivalent of the firm recovery of his parents) held his loneliness in check. This seems to be the psychological meaning of his refusal to commit suicide, first during adolescence and then at the time of his disenchantment with his wife, because he hoped to develop his mathematical understanding, that is, arrive at certainty.

—Ben-Ami Scharfstein, *The Philosophers: Their Lives and the Nature of Their Thought*

The Picasso of modern philosophy.

—Description of Russell by A. J. Ayer, the British apostle of logical positivism

. . . Honorable exercises in moral philosophy, but lacking in life and flesh. It is as if he is talking about counters moving in certain directions, and not people at all.

—Isaiah Berlin, on Russell's popular essays

Vomitive.

—Wittgenstein's opinion on the same subject

Will machines destroy emotions, or will emotions destroy machines?

—Russell, in *Skeptical Essays*

A "dog," a "bum," a "fifth columnist," an "avowed Communist."

    —Descriptions of Russell in the U.S. press, provoked by his liberal pronouncements in 1940

. . . This philosophizing wolf whose dinner jacket conceals all but the brutal instincts of a beast. Hatred, murder, the eat-one-another state, seem to me the fundamental ethical principles preached by this beast in philosopher's robes.

    —Description of Russell on Radio Moscow after one of his speeches had been broadcast in Russian on the BBC Overseas Service

Children go to school impressed with a belief that they have a right to be happy. . . . This is the perversion of the true religion, self-denial and obedience.

    —Rev. Edward Lyttleton, former headmaster of Eton, an opponent of Russell's educational principles

In the course of a public lecture, Russell claimed that it was not possible to break the rules of mathematics without disastrous consequences. Once a false mathematical statement was introduced, it was possible to prove anything. At this point a voice from the back of the crowd interrupted him: "If two multiplied by two is five, then you must be able to show that I am the Pope. Prove it!"

Without hesitation Russell replied: "If two multiplied by two is five, then four equals five. Subtract three from both sides, then one equals two. But you and the Pope are two, therefore you and the Pope are one."

Chronology of Significant Philosophical Dates

6th C B.C.	The beginning of Western philosophy with Thales of Miletus.
End of 6th C B.C.	Death of Pythagoras.
399 B.C.	Socrates sentenced to death in Athens.
c 387 B.C.	Plato founds the Academy in Athens, the first university.
335 B.C.	Aristotle founds the Lyceum in Athens, a rival school to the Academy.

324 A.D.	Emperor Constantine moves capital of Roman Empire to Byzantium.
400 A.D.	St. Augustine writes his *Confessions*. Philosophy absorbed into Christian theology.
410 A.D.	Sack of Rome by Visigoths heralds opening of Dark Ages.
529 A.D.	Closure of Academy in Athens by Emperor Justinian marks end of Hellenic thought.
Mid-13th C	Thomas Aquinas writes his commentaries on Aristotle. Era of Scholasticism.
1453	Fall of Byzantium to Turks, end of Byzantine Empire.
1492	Columbus reaches America. Renaissance in Florence and revival of interest in Greek learning.
1543	Copernicus publishes *On the Revolution of the Celestial Orbs*, proving mathematically that the earth revolves around the sun.

1633	Galileo forced by church to recant heliocentric theory of the universe.
1641	Descartes publishes his *Meditations*, the start of modern philosophy.
1677	Death of Spinoza allows publication of his *Ethics*.
1687	Newton publishes *Principia*, introducing concept of gravity.
1689	Locke publishes *Essay Concerning Human Understanding*. Start of empiricism.
1710	Berkeley publishes *Principles of Human Knowledge*, advancing empiricism to new extremes.
1716	Death of Leibniz.
1739–1740	Hume publishes *Treatise of Human Nature*, taking empiricism to its logical limits.
1781	Kant, awakened from his "dogmatic slumbers" by Hume, publishes *Critique of Pure Reason*.

Great era of German metaphysics begins.

1807   Hegel publishes *The Phenomenology of Mind*, high point of German metaphysics.

1818   Schopenhauer publishes *The World as Will and Representation*, introducing Indian philosophy into German metaphysics.

1889   Nietzsche, having declared "God is dead," succumbs to madness in Turin.

1921   Wittgenstein publishes *Tractatus Logico-Philosophicus*, claiming the "final solution" to the problems of philosophy.

1920s   Vienna Circle propounds Logical Positivism.

1927   Heidegger publishes *Being and Time*, heralding split between analytical and Continental philosophy.

1943   Sartre publishes *Being and Nothingness*, advancing

Heidegger's thought and instigating existentialism.

1953   Posthumous publication of Wittgenstein's *Philosophical Investigations*. High era of linguistic analysis.

Chronology of Russell's Life

1872   Russell born May 18 in Trelleck on
            the Welsh border.

1877   His father dies, leaving him and his
            brother as orphans. His grandfather,
            Lord Russell, successfully contests his
            father's will; Russell and his older
            brother Frank are brought up by
            their grandparents at Pembroke
            Lodge.

1878   His grandfather, twice prime minister,
            dies.

1883   Introduced to mathematics by his
            brother Frank.

1888   After being privately educated at

Pembroke Lodge, he attends London crammer to prepare for university exams.

1890   Wins scholarship to Trinity College, Cambridge.

1893   Wins first-class honors at mathematical honors examinations; abandons mathematics in favor of philosophy.

1894   Wins first-class degree in moral science (philosophy).

1894   Marries Alys Pearsall Smith, against wishes of his grandmother, Lady Russell.

1896   Publishes his first book, *German Social Democracy*.

1897   With G. E. Moore, rejects neo-Hegelian idealism as taught at Cambridge by J. M. E. Taggart.

1900   Meets Italian logician Giuseppe Peano at the International Congress of Philosophy in Paris.

1900–1901	Writes *The Principles of Mathematics* (not published until 1903).
c 1903–1913	Spends decade collaborating with Whitehead writing *Principia Mathematica*.
1903	Suddenly falls out of love with Alys.
1907	Stands at Wimbledon by-election in support of woman suffrage and free trade.
1910	Meets Lady Ottoline Morrell and begins an affair.
1911	Wittgenstein arrives at Cambridge. He quickly becomes Russell's pupil and protégé.
1912	Publishes *The Problems of Philosophy,* the first of his popular books. Wittgenstein appalled.
1914	Outbreak of World War I, Russell begins pacifist campaign.
1918	Sent to Brixton Prison for pacifist activities.
1920	Visits Bolshevik Russia.

1921	Marries Dora Black.
1927	Opens Beacon Hill School with Dora.
1931	Austrian logician Gödel proves mathematics to be incomplete.
1935	Divorce from Dora.
1936	Marries Patricia Spence.
1938–1944	Lives in the United States.
1942–1944	Writing *A History of Western Philosophy*, which is published in 1945 and soon becomes a best-seller, providing him with an income for the rest of his life.
1949	Marriage to Patricia Spence breaks up.
1950	Awarded Nobel Prize for literature.
1952	Fourth wedding at age seventy, this time to American Edith Finch, a marriage that would last until his death.
1958	Starts Campaign for Nuclear Disarmament.

1959	Arrested for civil disobedience, sent to Brixton Prison.
1960s	Campaigns against Vietnam War.
1970	Dies at ninety-seven.

Recommended Reading

Ray Monk, *Bertrand Russell: The Spirit of Solitude, 1872–1921* (Free Press, 1996). The first volume of Monk's superb, possibly definitive biography, which covers Russell's most significant philosophical years.

Ray Monk, *Bertrand Russell: The Ghost of Madness, 1921–1970* (Free Press, 2001). The concluding volume of Monk's great biography, covering the years when Russell was more of a public figure—though still producing a variety of philosophical works.

Bertrand Russell, *Autobiography* (Routledge, 2000). A lucid and entertaining account of his long and varied life, though its poise and clarity glosses over the occasional unresolved complexities.

Bertrand Russell, *A History of Western Philosophy* (Simon and Schuster, 1975). A lengthy but always reliable account of the Western philosophical tradition in its social context. Undoubtedly biased, but redeemed by lively and provocative wit.

Bertrand Russell, *The Principles of Mathematics* (Norton, 1996). Russell's first great work, originally published in 1903, which captures his enthusiasm for the ideas that would eventually lead him to write the *Principia Mathematica* with Whitehead.

Bertrand Russell, *The Problems of Philosophy,* 2nd ed. (Oxford University Press, 1998). Still one of the best introductions to the perennial questions that have provided the subject matter of philosophy.

Index

A NOTE ON THE AUTHOR

Paul Strathern has lectured in philosophy and mathematics and now lives and writes in London. A Somerset Maugham prize winner, he is also the author of books on history and travel as well as five novels. His articles have appeared in a great many publications, including the *Observer* (London) and the *Irish Times*. His own degree in philosophy was earned at Trinity College, Dublin.